God I Feel Modern Tonight

God I Feel Modern Tonight

poems from a gal about town

Catherine Cohen

ALFRED A. KNOPF · New York

2021

THIS IS A BORZOI BOOK
PUBLISHED BY ALFRED A. KNOPF

www.aaknopf.com

"poem I wrote after I asked you if cereal can expire"
first appeared in *Together in a Sudden Strangeness: America's
Poets Respond to the Pandemic*, edited by Alice Quinn
(Alfred A. Knopf, 2020).

Knopf, Borzoi Books, and the colophon are registered
trademarks of Penguin Random House LLC.

Library of Congress Cataloging-in-Publication Data
Names: Cohen, Catherine, [date] author.
Title: God I feel modern tonight :
poems from a gal about town / Catherine Cohen.
Description: First edition. | New York :
Alfred A. Knopf, 2021. | This is a Borzoi book
published by Alfred A. Knopf.
Identifiers: LCCN 2020020451 (print) |
LCCN 2020020452 (ebook) | ISBN 9780593318331 (hardcover) |
ISBN 9780593318348 (ebook)
Subjects: LCGFT: Poetry.
Classification: LCC PS3603.O3433 G63 2021 (print) |
LCC PS3603.O3433 (ebook) | DDC 811/.6—dc23
LC record available at https://lccn.loc.gov/2020020451
LC ebook record available at https://lccn.loc.gov/2020020452

Jacket illustration and design by Perry De La Vega

Manufactured in Canada
First Edition

Contents

poem I wrote after I crummed

(crum: to cry and cum at same time)

my beaded bag & I are going to CityMD
because I'm convinced I'm dying again
everyone who works here looks like they run a casino
but I still believe them
this morning at 2 p.m. I got a cold brew
and felt like falling in love
boys love to run down stairs fast
men love to date powerful women for 3–8 weeks
I love when someone is "surprise married"
that's when someone tells me they're married
and I'm like but you're my age
and they're like yeah
and I'm like that's surprising to me . . .

poem I wrote after I went to Tuscany to journal about my toxic guitar teacher

going swimming is an amazing way
to stop being on your phone
I woke up early as a cry for help but
there's no oranges in this sunrise
I was promised oranges
I was promised the upper west side
I woke up so early
and the lonely polo horses won't even come say hi
I can't believe I had sex in these woods
sex! the biggest, baddest thing you can do, baby!
sex with its slime and guts
and romance if you're drunk
it's nothing like swimming you know
when it's done

poem I wrote after I told you I was empathetic

I go to the CVS on 14th & 8th
and you've asked me not to contact you anymore
one time you were having a smoothie like it was 1998
and there was nothing I could do about it
your jawline is so perfect that I cannot stop
telling you to kill me even though you said please stop
asking me to kill you
a leaf just fell outside my window
remember when I tripped on the dance floor
and that guy who always talked about Ibiza
called me a fat whore?

I should have said I'm a leaf
I'm a leaf like I was in a play
like I was in something bigger than my body
I can't tell if my therapist is cool or just has short bangs

poem I wrote after I decided that all I need to do to be in a good mood is spend six hours alone in my apartment every day

when someone hates me I'm obsessed
I'm cosplaying as my ex
by watching a movie
in the middle of the day
my career goal is to raise a gorgeous
brooklyn-based toddler
whose friend will one day cast them
in an academy award–winning film as a joke
I also want to be the first woman
in ill-fitting pants to be in an episode
of Succession
I want to show up with a camel toe
and have everyone be like
wait . . .

God I Feel Modern Tonight

poem I wrote after I found out that alcohol is actually just sugar

I live in America and
there's only one good show on TV
I wake up early to watch the sunrise
anything can be political if you tweet about it
I can't imagine having children
I haven't even had sex with a doctor
sometimes I sigh so loud in public
that a stranger on the street will ask if I'm okay
I'm okay my work isn't good but it's online
and that's what counts

poem I wrote after I woke up at 6 a.m. as a joke

my beaded bag & I got stuck on the C train
& spoke to a guy who said he has the best
sound system in lower manhattan
in the future everyone will be 25 minutes late
to their 45 minute therapy session
in the future restaurants won't make you wait
for the whole party to arrive before they seat you
I can't wait to check my phone
I can't wait to hear my daughter's first podcast
I ask my therapist why should I want to grow
she says I will suffer less
what is she trying to prove?
an italian waiter once told me the
only thing that matters is the sound of the rain
did he even *want* to fuck me?

**poem I wrote after I looked at your jawline and
it ruined my life**

at this point if my pussy doesn't feel weird
that's when I start to worry
some of my closest friends have
chosen to go to weddings
instead of hanging around the city
listening to me complain about someone
I kissed in 2012
when someone is married I do take that personally
when someone is tall I love that shit
there's a german word for wanting
to burn down everything you own
but I guess I could just sublet my place

poem I wrote after I masturbated while wearing airpods

I just found out dog isn't short for something
it's actually just called a dog, which is fine with me
I'm in the kitchen alone, which is romantic in a way
anything can be romantic if you sigh a lot
one time I told this guy I loved him
and he said "I don't know what love is"
anyway he just got engaged

**poem I wrote after I went to the gym with
someone I had sex with**

sometimes being an adult means washing your hair
sometimes the only way to know
if someone is definitely straight
is if they instagram a building
sometimes I feel like
if I look at my phone
I will die
or even worse, not die

it's insane when you ask someone to give you space
and then they do

poem I wrote after I sent three guys the same nude

my dad is jewish & my mom is catholic
so I was confirmed catholic
but now the only holy trinity in my life
is yeast infection, diarrhea, period blood
do you like this?

**poem I wrote after I didn't drink for six days
and thought about starting a cult**

I have a disease where I never want
to get out of the uber
because then it means I have to be somewhere
for years I've been suffering from a serious addiction
to Adam Driver and Jason Schwartzman even
I think my crush hasn't texted me
because I'm out of town
but then again I never told him I was going out of town
what if I used my brain for good
instead of thinking about boys with swoopy hair all day?

**poem I wrote after you told me your ex is
"actually really cool"**

no one talks about this but in 2013
I inserted a tampon in the back seat of a car
on my way to a nickelback concert
I said I'd go to the concert
because my friend Ted asked me to
turns out I'm addicted to male attention
even when it's platonic
I don't like nickelback
I only like songs that sound like surfing
but then the lyrics are like "I wanna die"
I wish I were smart instead of on my phone

poem I wrote after you went down on me and then called me "dude"

whenever someone looks at me on the subway
I'm like okay they want to have raw dog sex with me
I think me ordering a coffee "to stay" at a café
could be the entire plot of a romcom
I've been trying
to come up with ideas for my screenplay
so I googled "things that happen to people"
and the first thing that came up
was a website called "list of bad things"
and the first thing on the list was
"your home is broken into and you are raped"
and I think that is definitely two bad things
I don't know I didn't make the website
I'm so confident and scared and certain
that seeing a tree through a window
is my religion. I hate feeling bad
I don't even like walking downhill
when someone hates me it hurts
my feelings of course

poem I wrote after I ruined the bathroom at Au Bon Pain

I haven't listened to a new song since college
& I'm not going to start now
the only kind of films I like are where a woman in a wig
tries to produce a male heir for her stoic husband
the only kind of music I like
is where a man with a long beard
whispers near a tree
oh no the handsome guy is trying to do comedy
oh no the polyamorous couple is taking a cooking class
the older I get the more I find
instagram to be an amazing place to watch
your camp friend's fiancé wakeboard

poem I wrote after I realized no one talks about that time the lululemon employee murdered her coworker in the store

I don't want to be your girlfriend
I just want to be a student of english literature
wandering home late drunk in autumn
and anyways I'm an awful roommate
I don't recycle don't repeat that
the other day
I was dry-swallowing my birth control pill
as I citi biked up the williamsburg bridge
and I was like okay . . .
I guess I am the voice of my generation

poem I wrote after I decided something was going on with the moon

a guy on the street
said I looked like I was studying
audio engineering in school
he told me he liked my outfit
he told me to have a cool day
I am googling how long a stroke lasts

poem I wrote after you ordered fried shrimp at the diner and I was like "gross" but really I was like "dang that sounds good"

I'm always horny
& looking for somewhere to charge my phone
The Paris Review came in the mail today
and I performed reading it
I can't write if no one is watching
I can't stop checking my pussy for weird bumps
one time I went to the doctor
and when she told me I'd gained 15 lbs
I was like that's a lot and she was just like yeah . . .

modern love poem

I should think more about the government
but I just want you to tell me
that fucking me
is the end of the world

poem I wrote last night when I couldn't go to sleep
because there are no sheets on my bed because
I perioded on my other sheets and cannot be
bothered to put new ones on

I'm sorry I friended your fiancé on facebook
I just meant to look at his profile pictures
I was on my phone
I haven't spoken to you in at least seven years
but you can't get engaged to your personal trainer
and not have me stalk him

**poem I wrote after I did the dishes in my
apartment and was like . . . okay I'm in a play**

my favorite sex position is
I'm splayed out on a canopy bed
silk sheets, it is raining
& my lover has just popped out
(braving the storm vibes)
to grab 2 kit kats
& a black cherry seltzer
people are addicted to being how they are

the first time I got fingered
was on a lawn chair
by a guy who said his favorite band
was Jason Mraz
*~life isn't about the breaths you take but the moments
    that take your breath away~*

poem I wrote after experiencing an amazing hangover

scientists are still trying to figure out
what childhood event
caused me to be attracted to men
who wear baseball hats that are barely
on top of their head
one time my ex-boyfriend broke up with me and
when we got back together
we made out next to a fountain and he said
"you've gotten better at that" and I said "at kissing?"
and he said "yeah"
and I laughed and felt very bad

bodies are hard and mine is soft and often in the way
you can tell me you like it a million times
some days I will believe you
and some days I will not I think the worst thing
is when you think someone is your friend
and then they tell you
they love jogging

poem I wrote after I told you about my joie de vivre

I'm sorry I never saw your play
theatre is yelling at people to leave rooms and/or
begging people to stay in rooms
New York is cool because you get to wait in line
to walk over a puddle

poem I wrote after I got scolded at the whole foods for stealing a meatball from the salad bar

I used to get mad at my ex-boyfriend
whenever it took him too long
to plug in my iphone charger
turns out if you listen to Lovefool by the Cardigans
for three days on repeat
you will actually get my personality
I just overheard a guy in my uber pool admit to having
"low-key misogyny issues"
over the phone. at least
I can make myself cum with my hand
Lifehack!

**poem I wrote after we enjoyed crying about how
we can't be together**

no one's ever been sad to leave Los Angeles
and I refuse to learn how to parallel park
one time I lied & said I wasn't going to date anymore &
went to a definitely cool roof party &
had seven beers & ran around asking everyone
"who is that tall person and what is his deal?"
you can't love someone else
until you love yourself JK

**poem I wrote after calling someone a
"darling of the scene"**

I'm sorry I bailed
on the yoga booty ballet class we signed up for
I did not sleep well last night
and am still reeling from the time
I slept with someone who didn't know
who Greta Gerwig is

**poem I wrote after seeing that guy from project
runway at the whole foods AGAIN**

I'm sorry I didn't text you back
about borrowing my adult-size tutu
for your sketch comedy show
I was on the L train trying to remember
how I knew the guy sitting
across from me turns out
it was from sex

poem I wrote after I read an article on why it is so hard to go up stairs

I just made eye contact with a stranger
while I burped
so loud for so long
while crossing the street like Frogger
the only video game I ever played was called
Mary Kate and Ashley: Magical Mystery Mall
it was fun to play because I could be thin
and blonde for a while
it would be nice to be thinner but
I have all the working parts
I don't want to get hit by a car at all

poem I wrote after I called myself the taylor swift of comedy

I am listening to a spotify playlist called "indie brunch"
while browsing the wikipedia page for "murder"
one time I drank so much I woke up in the hospital
and I still had to go to spanish class

poem I wrote after a stranger on youtube said
he wouldn't fuck me with someone else's cock

I just turned 25 yesterday
so now I am ¼ done with my life
I can't decide if I should get a $20 cheeseburger
or save up to buy a microwave
I would eat anything for more twitter followers
I went to the opening day of whole foods williamsburg
they let me throw the first pitch
I slung an organic leek into the soft paw
of a gray-haired tween
it is amazing that things
are not constantly falling on our heads
especially in Brooklyn, New York,
where everyone in the world lives

poem I wrote after I ordered a waffle as a side dish

I think about the girls my boyfriend kissed
before he knew I existed more
than I think about my friends and family and
I can't do a cartwheel
yesterday at rehearsal I told everyone
I could do the splits
and then ripped my urban outfitters pants in half
it was funny in a TV way but no one laughed

you say it is okay to be anxious
you say love is like a long worm

I think
I have a yeast infection

**poem I wrote after I asked my personal trainer
if he believed in god**

last night I went to a concert
and a girl younger than me
was wearing a t-shirt that said
"suck my ass" and I felt old
I know I'm not actually old
but it's fun to be like
haha I'm old
whenever I think someone looks cool I realize
they are just thin
jealousy is cool because it is like swallowing a house
that you just set on fire

poem I wrote after my therapist told me to have a drink

one time I misplaced a block
of cheddar cheese in my apartment
I wrote a facebook status about it
and it almost got a hundred likes
I found the block of cheese
45 minutes later on my bookshelf
I would read more if it were easier to hold a book up
while lying down they are too heavy

poem I wrote after I told you I was free bleeding at the improv show

I'm watching that catfish show on MTV
the host just told all the girls with eyeliner
that the person they have been sexting is fat
and now everyone is sad
one time I thought I was in love
because I was sad all the time
what if I wrote a poem about what love was lol

**poem I wrote after you helped me assemble my
new couch and then broke up with me on it**

the body is elastic
and I don't think it's embarrassing
that you bought a hat.
the body is elastic
and I like to run when that
brian eno song plays
if it's cold out
and I see the shape
of your name
on my phone.
the body is elastic
and love is boring but sex
is more of it and
your friend just
got one of those dogs that can't breathe
but they keep making them
even though it's like
a genetic thing?
anyways the point is I still love you
because I don't know what you're thinking
and because we refuse to talk about it
I remain in a good mood
because the performance hasn't
ended and I'm an incredible actress
because I think so

and feel so much all the time
and when I tire of this
there will be more of it
you're not the first
to give me a book
they haven't read

love poem for my british lover

in a past life I was a tycoon smoking
a cigar and you were my wife. I'm sorry
I never took you to Paris. But tonight
at the casino you promise me we'll stay
till 4 a.m. There's an old man
in the corner sipping noodle soup
and you ask me what I love
about that. Back in New York
I eat and sleep fine. I'm sad
about many different colored things
I turn into a paste. If I'm honest
I felt more in love that time
the Orthodox Jew I was dating
ran away from me when we saw his friend
in line to see the Gatsby remake at the Garden Theater.
Do you know a bunch of people
paid hundreds of dollars to watch a man
read the entirety of the Great Gatsby
out loud onstage?
Do you know I've never been
laughed out of a room for saying my favorite book
is Catcher in the Rye?
Do you know why I keep telling everyone
we're getting married in Paris
as a joke
in the spring?

every good song is named "dreams"

I wanted something to happen to me. My mouth
was so dry and running about some drummer
I spoke to for six minutes at a theater
on 54th street three weeks ago.

We were walking down Atlantic Avenue and
some kind of street zamboni was blowing litter
at my shins, whirring loud enough that when it stopped
I realized I was screaming

poem I wrote after you told me "I don't think you're as amazing as you think you are"

That summer I was so close to the city
there was no easy way to get in the water
I bruised my shins falling out of the canoe
I'd pulled to the center of the world

I'd have to muck through the slip
at the bottom of the pond
to let myself take time off
Nothing as a respite from nothing. How young

I felt so serious spelling out I Love You.
(and putting a period at the end)
so you would know I really meant it
I only meant it because I was lonely
but I don't see at all why that wouldn't count

Life is in the spaces between sex with you

at the bodega on Nostrand
I can see the reflection
of the shop behind me as
I look out the window

through aisles of potato chips,
variations on Cholula
over the radio a man croons
"Jazz Club: if you found us, you're in"

when it happens, poems are
poem-ier. songs are song-ier. heartbreak,
when it comes, and it will come,
is always new

oh god

it rained for six days straight in new york city
and I started telling everyone I want a boyfriend
the rain made me think I wanted a boyfriend
so what if I do
I accept I can't change you, I accept you're in rome,
I accept I've romanticized
your knowledge of music theory—
for all my talk of songs I'm much better at calculus,
geometry, noticing the way
you pull your sleeves up in the park.
all my fantasies revolve around a screen door,
red wine, the dirty projectors, stew in the summer,
rain as an excuse to do everything in excess,
sex that makes you hungry
for stew in the summer. I am
not the one who noticed
I only reveal what I really want in song—
a man in flannel with one hand
on the steering wheel
telling me something I won't remember
because it isn't memorable

it's worse than I thought

street signs don't know about you
the woman from belgium putting her hair up
in a ponytail doesn't know about you
the new starbucks on 15th and 9th sells pizza
sorry, flatbreads, beanies, tumblers?
there's an espresso station, a full-service bar,
gender-neutral bathrooms with slanted
fuck-me sinks that don't
know about you
and everyone in this starbucks
is acting like my being in this starbucks
isn't the craziest thing in the world,
acting like today has anything to do
with not being the day you leave
I call you, wine-drunk and humid
glowing night-bright and wanting
you to respect my time
telling myself I'm telling not begging
I'm a communicator, I'm mature,
I'm buying kettle chips and wheat beer
with a credit card
there's nothing wrong with feeling on fire
if it's embarrassing it's probably good

Italy

I've been neglecting my poetry group
but that's just the start of it.
Sheila Heti says her depression was a wall
that kept her from seeing the world.
I dreamt my ex had a "face disease"
This vacation is the longest day of my life and
even here the water smells like Arkansas,
the catfish think in Italian
I wonder if Joe Bolton
ever wished he hadn't said
I love you
as he wondered how it was
we came to live in cities.

I got nervous and ordered
the cow stomach at dinner
Solitude
A sofa bed
The catfish & their Italian thoughts

It's not fun being by yourself
& it's not fun being with someone else
that's not an original thought
which just makes it true

**The night we met you kissed me in a closet and
I slapped you and told you to ruin my life**

all I do is eat and drink and fuck
and think about fucking you
and fucking you is remembering
the version of me that got off
just at the thought that I could
in front of another person
this isn't romantic
this is some kind of sick
cosmic experiment
to take me away from my work
I'm not a fan
of anything
I don't care about rope or sand or
winged beasts
my god I could die
and will
if you look at me
while you hang up the curtains
you pulled off the rod
the last time
you looked at me

**There's no such thing as overreacting,
it's called reacting, darling!**

a doctor told me my ass
is scientifically weak
and that's why my hip hurts
oh that's why my hip hurts
that's why I'm calling you
to ask if you miss me
which is the best way
to know you don't.
god I feel modern tonight
god I feel present
I just watched a nine-minute video
where a girl named Nicole
that I've never met
tells me how to make a messy bun
with just a clip
you tell me there's no halves with me
you tell me there's pearls in my gut
I tell you there's a play about us
you ask what it's really about.
my friend cuts my hair
my friend brings me flowers to put
in a vase my friend made me
this bay window makes me
happy to be sad

James says there's a difference
between humor and satire
and that it's technically not a bay window
if it doesn't extend to the floor

the void

last night I told ian I loved him
and then he made me squirt
four times just like
in the movies
I'm on a plane to london
to meet aaron at a fuck hotel
I don't feel bad
about sending scotty
the nudes I take
pills to feel
less like a protagonist
drink orange wine to
feel more like one
I live in new york so I know
about joan didion
she says the void is like a snake
you can't kill
so you better keep your eye on it
but when you bite my neck
it feels so
good

**poem I wrote after I downloaded The Sims
at age 28 during quarantine**

In Paris we couldn't figure out how to get
to the Arc de Triomphe so we went to Sephora
we had pink wine by the water
and you told me you didn't think
anyone ever died from getting fingered too hard
that night I got McDonald's
and watched 13 Reasons Why alone
on my laptop in Paris
I never told anyone that
a few weeks ago I broke a glass in my apartment and
I was too lazy to clean it up so
I kind of just pushed it into a corner
and now every few days I step on a tiny piece of glass
it doesn't hurt it's just part of my new lifestyle
can you die from being in a bad mood?

poem I wrote after I had a dream Jessica Simpson took me "under her wing"

I cut my boyfriend's hair on Instagram Live
and all I got was a sense of community
and this rush of adrenaline
Spotify tells me I can work from home with Vivaldi
what's it called when you dread the end
of something before it starts?
we're out of toilet paper and I just ordered
a bejeweled headband online
it's coming Friday is it sexy
how much I hate being alone?

I ask my boyfriend if he wants to marry me
we've been drinking a new milk made from peas
I tell him I would say no if he asked
he says that's okay it's a big decision

I miss the food from Starbucks
I miss the shuttle at LAX
I miss crying in Italy outside
listening to Norman Fucking Rockwell on repeat
counting down the hours
till you'd pick me up at Gatwick
not as a surprise, because I asked you to
which upset you
because you were going to,
whether or not I asked

**poem I wrote after I listened to my Spotify
top songs of 2019 and it undid all the work
I did in therapy last year**

doctors really broke the mold
when they invented antidepressants
that make you feel worse
a pill that makes it harder to cum?
honey, where do I sign?!
I tried unlearning jealousy in 2015
I tried barre class
next year I'm going to buy something
and feel better for 12 minutes

poem I wrote after my lover quoted Zoolander towards me

If you don't have crippling anxiety you aren't modern
you're a pioneer woman
churning butter in your bonnet,
having 12 kids near a wagon et al.
sometimes I feel so sharp but my body is so soft
is there an app for that?
I miss the simple things:
emailing someone named Jen,
crying about different types of love on the plane,
saying "my career is my boyfriend" over and over again
until blood comes out of all my holes,
figure skating.
I just want to go to an institution
where they charge you $12
to add the meat chicken
and tell you I once had a therapist tell me
you can't gain weight
if you don't put food in your mouth

**poem I wrote after I opened a canned wine
upon receiving your email**

we go for a jog and I ask if you think we're dead
like a stoner
I don't like weed
because it makes me think I don't have legs
but I keep trying it every two years
before a massive panic attack
my favorite diet is not eating sugar
but liquor doesn't count
I'm going to do sober January
which means I don't drink
for the first four days of January and then I forget
I love the idea of playing chess
I love the egg bites at Starbucks
I had a dream I fucked Eminem "reverse cowgirl" style
on a beach in another country
If I die I want to be surrounded by everyone I love
and as I breathe my last breath
I'll ask everyone if my hair looks better
half up
or full down

poem I wrote after I asked my friend if her new boyfriend cares about me

I'm wearing jeans to punish myself unfortunately
I just walked into the other room
to make you pause your video game
so I could tell you that I think
if I read more I'll be in a better mood
today we filmed ourselves having sex and then got upset
because I thought I looked too big
and you thought you looked too small
then we went to watch the sunset
which is a nice thing to do
my big plan is to lose weight
by only eating cucumbers
cucumbers for meals only
my therapist says it's so important right now
to be gentle
lately it's so fucking impossible to talk to her
which is the thing
I am paying to do
the river is low enough that I can go walk around it
and skip rocks
which is a nice thing to do
even as I finish this poem
I'm mad at myself for not having started
another one yet

**poem I wrote after another exquisite morning
on my phone**

why is a bagel with butter so good? it should go viral
dieting is about eating as many eggs as you can
until you cry because you miss life before all the eggs
I love eating but I love drinking too please
don't put me in a box
should I intermittently fast or intuitively eat
or just continue to think about
food when I'm eating and
when I'm not eating for the rest
of my years
on earth
I'm beginning to suspect
I'm not going to drop the 12 lbs
I've been trying to lose
for the past fourteen years but who knows
one time in college my boyfriend
said he needed time to ruminate
and I was like what does that mean
and he explained it to me in the dining hall
now I get to have sex with you whenever I want
and when I'm out of town
I watch porn on my phone
and they say women can't have it all????????grow up

poem I wrote after I asked you if cereal can expire

there's a pandemic and I think my arms are fat
I used to worry I had vaginismus
but it turns out I just wasn't attracted to my ex
I put the wrong kind of gas
in the car and hate being alone
everything I do is on my computer,
which already feels like a word from the past
my children will type before they can walk
when I say children I feel like a painting,
like a Victorian woman
sent to be by the sea with her ailments,
which isn't not what's happening
upstate we have near constant sex and eat string cheese
I tell my therapist the rules
of Love Island and we unearth
that I feel like an islander trapped in the villa
wondering how things will be different
back on the outside
there is no world now but I still feel like
there must be some fabulous party
going on somewhere
everyone wearing shawls without me
smoking cigarettes with those long things
what are those? I miss feeling alive
by which I mean crying about my perfect life
and boys who don't know how to dress themselves,

who tell me they wish my bathroom
was farther from my bed
so they could look at my ass
for longer when I walk away
I keep asking you if you think we are dead up here
the sky is brilliant and the playground is empty
parts of your house are warmer than others
and we sleep in the cold spots, holding each other close

**poem I wrote after the new taylor swift album
came out thank god**

I haven't seen the sun in four days
and my dad just said he was proud of me
for finishing the leftovers
mailing letters is a great way
to feel like you're from before
when no one could google you & see
that you did a capella in college
one time I wanted so bad
to fall in love that I did it
what's it called when you have a sixth sense
that your ex is engaged?

poem I wrote after I had the strangest urge to confide in dear friends beneath starlight

I just took a pregnancy test to feel alive
and all I got was piss on my hands
I don't think I'd take my daughter
to get her nails done
if I were a mother
she can do that with her friends
if she wants
I'd like to have kids at 35
so I can start wearing graceful linen sacks
and calling everyone "darling"
I'd like to wear lipstick
and lean on a built-in bookcase
and tell you I like Helen Frankenthalther
and did you know that's her painting
on the Renata Adler novel I told you to read
the one I never finished
because I needed to have sex
with someone who lived on
the Upper West Side
can you grab some ice?
I like ice in my wine

poem I wrote after I texted my therapist that I'm not pregnant

all this hair grows out of the mole on my face
and I've got an ulcer from being alive
I'm so smart and beautiful
and terrible and horny
someone who called me a cunt online
just liked my tweet about feminism
but if I think about you laughing at six flags
I still feel so in love with the whole world
and that day we waited so long
to sit in the front car
that by the time it was our turn
it was night and dark and raining
but we still got on the ride

poem I wrote after I tried to write a tweet about sparkling water

I've got a disease where I haven't watched
an entire feature film since the aughts
do you like how I said "aughts"?
you don't see that every day!
I've never been to a sex party
but one time I made fun of this girl
for bringing deviled eggs to an event
and then I ate six of them.
humiliation, satisfaction,
a long walk home in spring.
I love sex and I love before it—
the double vodka soda leg touch
Is it possible to miss everything at once?

**poem I wrote after I took a photo of my tits with
a self-timer alone like an adult**

I don't want to turn 29
but it's better than the alternative
I'm tall for my age
and love buying diet coke
years ago I dated this guy in a blue sweater
who was horny to get down on one knee
but I needed to fuck someone
in the bathroom of a divebar in Bushwick
that I later referred to as "finger ass guy"
I'm very interested in Victorian literature
and why my left breast is so much
bigger than my right
whenever someone has a vase
or something in their home
I'm always like where did you get that?
did you wake up one morning
and walk to the open air market?
did the cerulean catch your eye?
did you pay in cash?
errands are so glamorous
before I've done them
I'm so in love with the grocery store
with asking you to grab the balsamic vinegar
with watching you eat
the stem of the strawberry

like a party trick and we're
the only ones invited
we've gone full cartoon-mode
wearing the same outfit every day
for the rest of our lives
waking up and having coffee
complaining and getting over it
you're surprised when I tell you I pray
but I like the idea of wanting something
all the way
into space

**poem I wrote after I made you tell me I was sexy
four times today**

I'm finding quarantine to be an amazing time
to revert to the basest, most vile
version of myself I've worked years
to outgrow
I'm reading a book about the guy
who discovered the color "mauve"
and googling vintage wallpaper
don't tell me what day it is
I've never been patient
I don't know how to "let something go"
people love encouraging self-care
until it's inconvenient for them
everyone on twitter is upset and that's the point
one time I had a trainer who was like
instead of having four drinks in one night
you should have four drinks in one week
and I was like yeah
that's definitely an amazing idea

boys love getting haircuts
boys love analogies
boys love arguing and calling it philosophy
this guy who wronged me just liked my comment
on our mutual friend's Instagram I'm almost
thirty

road trip poem #3

in LA we got naked & swam in the ocean
we ate cured meats & carrots
& sat in the back of a red pickup truck
like we were in a film where two old friends fight
& wrestle their way into a hug
heave-sobbing as the dust settles
I want to be famous for being the first person
who never feels bad again

road trip poem #9

I just zoned out while a married person told me
they know of an amazing banjo player I think
I don't care about fruit or anything sweet
that isn't chocolate lava cake served
on a white tablecloth at a restaurant
you get to go to because someone else
is in town. one time in LA a wealthy man
bought me a deconstructed cobb salad &
told me I should never take a job for money
I think he has a pied-à-terre
I would love to be in a good mood in america

road trip poem #12

sara says her art friends in philly
aren't happy and they aren't even close
I wonder if I should get a dishwasher
yesterday we drove through south dakota,
minnesota, wisconsin, we pulled over
right where james wright
saw those lonely horses
& I tell you I'd been thinking about his
hammock poem where he says
he wasted his life because we saw the sun
reflecting off that buffalo dung in yellowstone
which was overrated then amazing
how deep does the ground go by the way?
that night we had sex under the stars
and I peed in the wrong place after
do you think they will know it was me?
I do my best work
when I'm hungover and mortified
no one ever got any good ideas
from feeling perfect

road trip poem #17

I'm jealous of everyone
and wouldn't change a thing
every time we have sex I tell you
it's one for the record books
and you say something can't be special
if everything is. boys love drumming on stuff
boys love taking their shirt off with one hand
oh my god experience
whatever pleasure you can in this life
for example I'm at mcdonald's right now

road trip poem #20

I think a company that mailed me free
sunglasses just unfollowed me on instagram
we agree that watching the sun set
is better than watching it rise
after it's up you have to just like
 . . . do a whole day
I've gone full-tilt suburban mom
leaving my coffee on top of the car
as we speed off
unbuttoning my jeans as we drive
wishing I was somewhere else for a second
and then changing my mind

A Note About the Author

CATHERINE COHEN, a native of Houston, Texas, is a comedy sensation who has a residency at Joe's Pub and hosts a weekly show at Club Cumming in NYC; she also cohosts the popular podcast about dating, boys, and sex, *Seek Treatment*. She has been featured in *The New York Times*, *Vogue*, and *The Village Voice*, and was named Best Newcomer at the Edinburgh Fringe Festival in 2019. Her many film and TV credits include a role in Michael Showalter's *The Lovebirds* and Season 3 of *High Maintenance* on HBO. Follow her while you're young @catccohen on Instagram.

A Note on the Type

This book was set in Janson, a typeface long thought to have been made by Anton Janson, a practicing typefounder in Leipzig during the years 1668–1687. However, these types are actually the work of Nicholas Kis (1650–1702), a Hungarian, who likely learned his trade from the Dutch master Dirk Voskens. The type is an excellent example of the influential and sturdy Dutch types that prevailed in England up to the time William Caslon (1692–1766) developed his own incomparable designs from them.

Composed by North Market Street Graphics,
Lancaster, Pennsylvania

Printed by Friesens,
Altona, Manitoba

Designed by Cassandra J. Pappas